Developing Optimism

Teaching Children the Value of Positive Thinking

by Barb Rumson

Fearon Teacher Aids
A Division of Frank Schaffer Publications, Inc.

Body Illustrations: Jeanette Courtin and Steve Sullivan
Cover Illustration: Jeanette Courtin

Editors: Pamela K. Jennett, Hanna Otero, Christine Hood
Book Design: Riley Wilkinson
Graphic Artists: Carol Arriola, Drew R. Moore

Fearon Teacher Aids products were formerly manufactured and distributed by American Teaching Aids, Inc., a subsidiary of Silver Burdett Ginn, and are now manufactured and distributed by Frank Schaffer Publications, Inc. FEARON, FEARON TEACHER AIDS, and the FEARON balloon logo are marks used under license from Simon & Schuster, Inc.

FE11028 — Developing Optimism Grades 4-6
© **Fearon Teacher Aids**
A Division of Frank Schaffer Publications, Inc.
23740 Hawthorne Boulevard
Torrance, CA 90505-5927

Table of Contents

A Rule for Life

by John Wesley

Do all the good you can,
By all the means you can,
In all the ways you can,
In all the places you can,
At all the times you can,
To all the people you can,
As long as ever you can.

Introduction

As students enter school, they bring with them learned behaviors. Some children will have optimistic attitudes about their abilities and the world around them. Others will have already developed negative attitudes. Research shows that optimistic children do better in all areas of their endeavors.

This workbook contains 12 lessons that will help students acquire skills to develop and maintain optimism. Each lesson begins with insights. These are brief statements about the lesson to follow. These insights can be shared on an overhead projector, displayed as a poster, or reserved for your eyes only. The lesson continues with a short introduction, followed by the main activity. The activity concludes with a section called "anchoring." This last phase is vital in order to solidly establish and practice the newly-acquired skill. Each section also includes extension activities that feature ideas for integrating language arts, poetry, art, science, social studies, and math. Each lesson follows the same format.

The lessons are set up in a continuum so that there is a progression of skills that will lead to increased optimism and potential success. The following provides an idea of how this progression is handled:

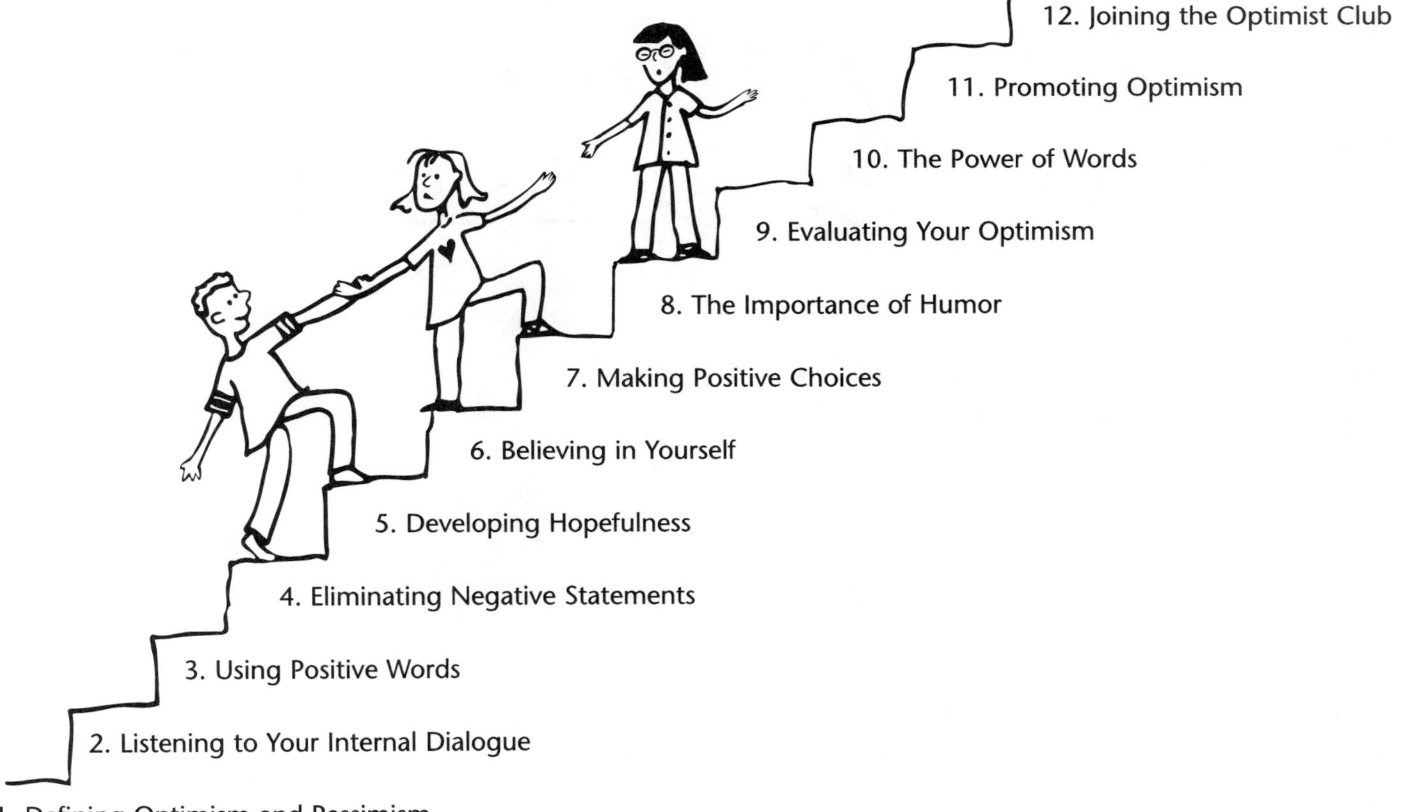

Students need guidance in using these skills. Through shared insights, discussions, and lesson plans, students will come to understand how and why a positive attitude can influence their lives. Once mastered, these skills will help students make optimistic choices. Students will conclude that a positive attitude affects how they feel about themselves and the world around them.

At the back of the book you will find four award certificates. You can pass these out to students when you notice an improvement in their attitudes, or you can allow students to award the certificates to their peers. Either way, continue to emphasize the benefits of a good attitude.

As an educator, you have the opportunity to help your students deal positively with the unexpected. You can encourage them to develop self-confidence and accept challenges with enthusiasm. Your classroom can be a positive environment that allows optimism to thrive. Start developing optimism today!

Optimist or Pessimist?

Lesson 1

Materials

Teacher copy of "Oliver and Pete" (pages 9 and 10)

Student copies of "Discussion Questions" (page 11)

Student copies of "Changing Your Word Scenery" (page 12)

Colored chalk: red and blue

Objective: Students will show that they understand the meaning of the words *optimism* and *pessimism.*

Time Required: 45 to 60 minutes

Insights

Start each day by making a positive remark about yourself.

Stop every few hours and give yourself a pat on the back.

Change your negative thoughts and you will change your perceptions.

Try to be constructive instead of destructive.

Introduction

Begin the lesson by asking students if they know anyone who is sometimes grumpy. Discuss the following questions:

1. How do you detect grumpiness?
2. How do grumpy people affect us?
3. Are grumpy people fun to have around?
4. Are negative people a good influence when there is a job to be done?
5. How does their mood spoil everyone else's fun?

Brainstorm words that describe negative people. Write these on the chalkboard. In red chalk, write the word *pessimist* on top of these words. Then continue with these questions:

6. How do we respond to people that are positive?
7. Are positive people easy to get along with?
8. Do positive people get things done?
9. Is happiness infectious?

Ask students to describe people they like to be around. Write these words or phrases in another column and write the word *optimist* at the top of the list in blue chalk. Have students read all the pessimist words. Then have them read all the optimist words. Have students compare and contrast the lists. Would they rather be friends with an optimist or a pessimist? Why?

Lesson 1

Optimist or Pessimist?

Activity

Read the story "Oliver and Pete" on pages 9 and 10. Ask students to determine who is the optimist and who is the pessimist.

Anchoring

Use the story to answer the following questions. First, ask for specific examples from the story. Then ask for more general examples from students' own experiences.

1. Does being pessimistic make things harder for the pessimist? Why or why not?
2. How does a pessimist make others feel?
3. How does an optimist make others feel?
4. How does being a pessimist affect one's performance?
5. How does being an optimist affect one's performance?
6. Why would you have more friends if you were an optimist?

Pass out copies of "Discussion Questions" to small student groups. Invite groups to discuss these questions about the story.

Then have students complete the "Changing Your Word Scenery" worksheet as part of the anchoring for Lesson One.

Name ____

Oliver and Pete

Oliver had a big smile on his face as he stopped his bicycle near his friend Pete.

"Hi, Pete," he said. "This is the day we start our big project. Let's make a plan. There's a book in the library on our topic that would give us a lot of information. I want to get it out today."

"What are you so excited about?" replied Pete. "I'm already having a lousy day. I don't want to talk about our stupid project. We don't need to plan."

Pete made a quick grab for the handlebars of his bike, but he lost his grip. The bicycle fell. "Darn. See, I told you. It just isn't any good. I'm doomed."

Pete's face was scrunched up. He gave his bicycle a kick and sat down.

"Come on, Pete," said Oliver. "Things will get better, you'll see."

"Leave me alone. You're always giving me that junk. It's not going to be a good day. It's just going to get worse. I know it." Pete's voice was getting louder and louder.

"Ah, come on, we have lots to do at school. I want to get to the library and get that book for our project." Oliver pushed off on his bicycle and left Pete.

"You know what?" Pete called as he got on his bike and peddled after Oliver. "You have a problem. You're always trying to rush me into doing things and I'm tired of it."

Oliver was at the bicycle racks securing his lock. Pete pushed his bicycle in beside Oliver's.

"See, we're late," said Pete, scowling at Oliver. "The kids are all here. I bet they won't let us get in the game."

"I'm not playing today. I told you I want to check out a book that would be awesome for our project," Oliver said.

"Listen, Oliver, we don't have to start our stupid project today. We've got lots of time."

Pete started toward the group of students playing in the field. "I bet they don't let me play," he said. "It's all your fault, Oliver. You made us late."

Pete turned back and looked for Oliver.

Lesson 1

Oliver moved away from Pete and started to walk toward the school doors. Pete followed after him.

"No one is going to take out that lousy book," Pete said. "Who would want that stupid book anyway?"

Oliver kept walking. "I want to go to the library and get that book before someone else gets it. You can go and play. Go on. I'll get the book for us."

"See! You're trying to make me feel guilty. You always make me feel like you're doing everything. You're always causing problems with your planning-ahead ideas."

Pete walked away. Oliver shrugged. He continued to the library without Pete.

Name ______________________________

Discussion Questions

1. Who was the optimist in the story "Oliver and Pete"?
2. Who was the pessimist?
3. Who made threatening remarks?
4. Do you think making pessimistic remarks made Pete feel better?
5. How did it make Oliver feel when Pete made these remarks about him?
6. Is it good to be a pessimist? Why or why not?
7. Are pessimists really PESTimists sometimes?
8. Without using real names, write a story about a time when you encountered a pessimist.

Lesson 1

Name ______________________________

Changing Your Word Scenery

Directions: Write the opposite of each word listed below. Find these new words in the puzzle. The remaining letters will spell out a message.

O	P	T	I	M	I	S	T	C	C
O	R	G	A	N	I	Z	E	D	O
E	A	C	A	R	I	N	G	L	O
H	C	S	I	N	C	E	R	E	P
A	T	T	E	N	T	I	V	E	E
P	I	H	E	L	P	F	U	L	R
P	C	E	B	R	A	T	E	C	A
Y	A	C	T	I	V	E	H	A	T
F	L	E	X	I	B	L	E	N	I
T	H	A	N	K	F	U	L	G	V
D	E	P	E	N	D	A	B	L	E
R	E	S	P	E	C	T	F	U	L
C	O	M	M	I	T	T	E	D	E

pessimist ______________________

inflexible ______________________

uncooperative ______________________

unhelpful ______________________

insincere ______________________

inattentive ______________________

uncaring ______________________

unorganized ______________________

disrespectful ______________________

thankless ______________________

uncommitted ______________________

passive ______________________

undependable ______________________

unhappy ______________________

impractical ______________________

Message: __ __ __ __ __ __ __ __ __ __ __   __ __ __ __ __ __ __ !

Extension Activities

Art

Tell students that a monogram is a design made with the initials of a name. Ask them to make their own monogram designs. Encourage them to embellish their letters and use their favorite colors.

Language Arts

- Have students look up the words *optimist* and *pessimist* in the dictionary and write out the definitions. Ask students to list some examples of times when someone they know was an optimist, then list some examples of situations in which someone was a pessimist.
- A tall tale is a story in which certain qualities in a character are exaggerated to outrageous proportions. Share *American Tall Tales* by Adrien Stoutenberg (Viking Press, 1976) or *Tall Tale America* by Walter Blair (University of Chicago Press, 1987) with the class. Invite students to write tall tales of their own using a truly optimistic or a truly pessimistic person as the main character.
- Many people believe that handwriting can reveal a lot about a person. Invite students to look up information about *graphology*, the study of handwriting. Have them read books about graphology, such as *Graphology for Beginners* by Richard Craze (Trafalgar Square Publishing, 1995). Can handwriting reveal whether a person is optimistic or pessimistic? How? What are some special signs?
- Ask students to research calligraphy and do some fancy writing of their names and those of their classmates. Try sharing a few books on calligraphy, including *Calligraphy* by Catherine Nichols (Troll Associates, 1999) and *The Art of Calligraphy: A Practical Guide to the Skills and Techniques* by David Harris (Dorris Kindersley, 1995). If you have a class computer, students can also experiment with typing their names in various fonts.

Math

Make a graph to record your class optimism and pessimism "scores" for a week. When someone hears an optimistic comment, he or she can mark it on the graph and increase the optimism score. If someone hears a pessimistic comment, he or she can record this as well. Discuss whether the week was optimistic or pessimistic, and why?

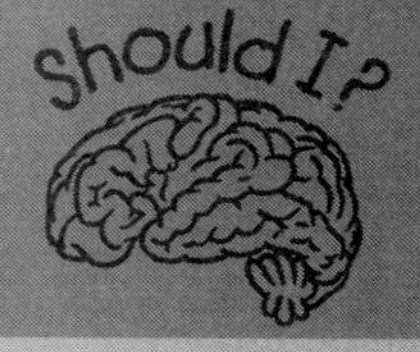

Lesson 2

Heady Dialogue

Materials

Student copies of "The Voice in Your Head" (page 16)

Objective: Students will define internal dialogue and understand why it is important to maintain optimism.

Time Required: 30 to 40 minutes

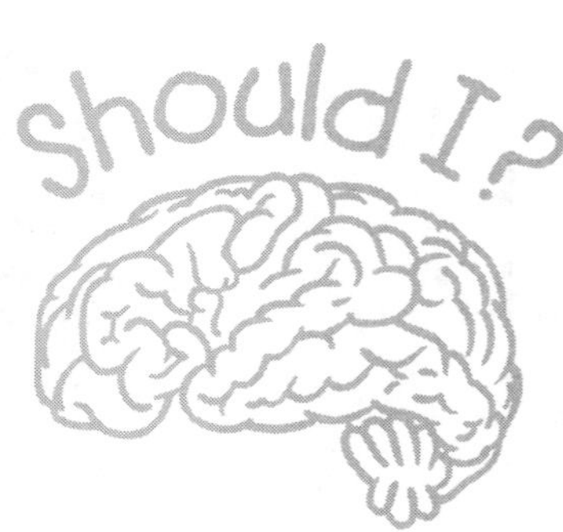

Insights

Learn to rehearse success in your mind.

Starting your day by focusing on positive internal dialogue will directly affect your attitude.

We can change unwanted and negative thoughts with positive strategies.

Internal dialogue can help you solve difficult problems as you consider all the consequences.

Introduction

Introduce this lesson by asking students if they sometimes talk to themselves while trying to solve problems. Write *internal dialogue* on the chalkboard. Explain that when we have conversations with ourselves, we are engaging in internal dialogue. Discuss the following questions:

1. When do you use internal dialogue?
2. Is it useful to solve problems this way?
3. How does this type of inner dialogue keep you calm?
4. How does it keep you out of trouble?
5. Can you give examples of situations in which internal dialogue can be advantageous?

Heady Dialogue

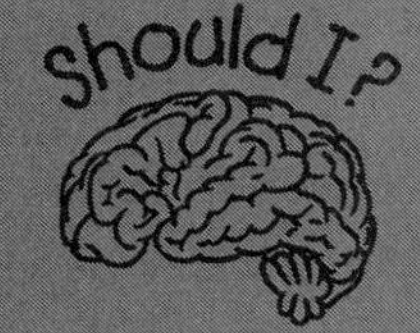

Activity

Place students in pairs. Give each pair of students a copy of "The Voice in Your Head" worksheet. Emphasize that none of the situations are directed at any particular student, but students should imagine that the situations involve them. Read the directions on the worksheet with students and allow them to complete the activity with their partners.

Anchoring

After all statements are read and students record their responses, ask each student pair to share their responses with the class. Pay special attention to responses in which the students used internal dialogue to affirm or negate the information they received. Discuss the following questions:

1. Does internal dialogue have benefits?
2. How can internal dialogue help you solve a problem?
3. Can internal dialogue help you to remain neutral?

Remind the class that using internal dialogue is like having a true friend to talk to all the time.

You KNOW you can do it!

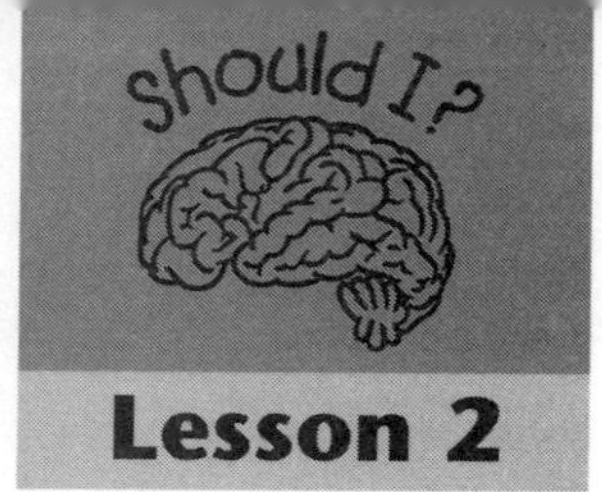

Lesson 2

Name ______________________________

The Voice in Your Head

Directions: Work with a partner. One partner reads the situation and then records a prediction about what his or her partner was thinking as the comment was being read. Partners can take turns reading and recording, then discuss the results together.

Situation One: Did you hear about the plans to go rock climbing? The school even hired a special rock climbing instructor. Isn't that great? But only six students will be selected to go. I guess that leaves you out. You're the biggest troublemaker in class. There's no chance of you going.

Predicted response: ______________________________

____

Situation Two: We're taking a vote on what kind of volunteering we're going to do this term. You probably don't want to do anything anyway, so it doesn't matter if you vote. You're never interested in anything. Why are you so lazy?

Predicted response: ______________________________

Situation Three: Hey, would you be my partner on the computer? I want to work with you because you always get good grades. Maybe if you work with me some of your smartness will rub off on me.

Predicted response: ______________________________

____

Situation Four: Why don't you look where you are going? You almost knocked me down. I know you did it on purpose, so don't even try to apologize. You think it's funny, don't you? You're always trying to get me into trouble.

Predicted response: ______________________________

____

Situation Five: Whose drawing is this? Is this yours? Wow, this is really good! You never told me you could draw. I wish I could draw as well as you can. Could you show me how you do it?

Predicted response: ______________________________

____

Extension Activities

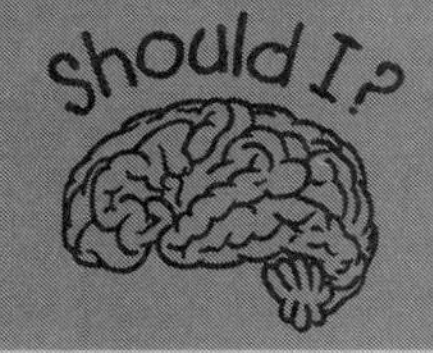

Drama

A fable is a story in which the characters learn a lesson. Usually the main characters are animals with human characteristics. Ask students to research a fable and turn it into a short play that can be acted out in front of the class. Here are some books of interest about fables:

Aesop's Fables by Aesop (Stern Sloan Publishers, 1977)

Friedman's Fables by Edwin H. Friedman (Gilford Press, 1990)

Language Arts

- Ask each student to imagine that someone has knocked on his or her door and announced, "You've just won one million dollars!" Have students write about this situation. What would be going through their heads at the time? What would they do with the money? In what ways would it positively or negatively change their lives?
- Discuss the following idioms with students:

  Look before you leap!

  Don't put all your eggs in one basket.

  It's no use crying over spilt milk.

  The early bird catches the worm.

Encourage students to draw posters that illustrate the ideas behind these sayings.

Lesson 3

Words That Work For You

Materials

Student copies of "Words That Work" game board (page 20)

Place markers, one die, a dictionary, and a thesaurus for each group

Student copies of "Magic Words of Success" (page 21)

Objective: Students will acquire a working vocabulary of positive words to use as an alternative to negative phrases.

Time Required: 45 minutes

Insights

You can be cheerful even when you are not happy.

To join the positive revolution, your thoughts should be directed by positive words.

Using positive words can help you overcome feelings of depression.

Self-improvement means changing yourself in a positive way.

Being positive and happy is our goal. Using the right words can point us in the right direction.

Introduction

Discuss with students how positive thoughts and ideas promote good health by lowering stress levels. Ask them to think about and share the following:

1. What are words that make you feel good?
2. What are words that make you feel bad?
3. What are words that relax you?
4. What are words that make you feel anxious?
5. Do some words make you feel sad or hurt?
6. Do certain words make you fearful?

Words That Work For You

Lesson 3

Activity

Divide the class into groups of three. Hand out a "Words That Work" game board, place markers, a die, a dictionary, and a thesaurus to each group. Read the directions with students and allow them to play the game.

Anchoring

After groups have played the game, come together as a class to discuss the following questions:

1. Have you found any words that affect you?
2. Are there words that have strong positive value?
3. Are there words that have strong negative value?
4. How do you feel when you use positive words?

To reinforce the use of these words, ask students to complete the word puzzle on the "Magic Words of Success" worksheet.

Beautiful words make a remarkable poem. Do beautiful words also make a beautiful person?

Lesson 3

Name ____

Words That Work Game Board

This game allows you to practice using the synonyms of positive words and finding the antonyms of negative words. Have a dictionary and thesaurus handy to help you check your answers.

Directions: Work in groups of three. Players take turns rolling the die and moving up the "Words That Work" game board. Players must use the correct antonym or synonym to move on. If you miss the word, you do not advance. The first person to reach 25 is the winner.

21 HOPELESS antonym	**22 STABLE** synonym	**23 CONFIDENT** synonym	**24 HUMOROUS** synonym	**25 SAD** antonym
20 CHEERFUL synonym	**19 GENEROUS** synonym	**18 FAIL** antonym	**17 PESSIMISTIC** antonym	**16 UNMOTIVATED** antonym
11 INFLEXIBLE antonym	**12 INACCURATE** antonym	**13 SUCCEED** synonym	**14 GRATEFUL** synonym	**15 FOCUS** synonym
10 COURAGE synonym	**9 SLOW** antonym	**8 OPTIMISTIC** synonym	**7 INTELLIGENT** synonym	**6 HOPEFUL** synonym
1 UNPREPARED antonym	**2 SINCERE** synonym	**3 DEPRESSED** antonym	**4 NEGATIVE** antonym	**5 EAGER** synonym
START HERE				

Name ____________________________________

Lesson 3

Magic Words of Success

Directions: Mark out the following words in the puzzle below. The remaining letters will spell out a message in the spaces provided.

Abilities	**Intelligence**	**Value**	**Motivate**	**Coping**
Alternatives	**Choice**	**Challenge**	**Useful**	**Eager**
Accomplishment	**Stable**	**Caring**	**Goals**	**Belief**
Solutions	**Humor**	**Hopeful**	**Friendship**	**Praise**

a	c	c	o	m	p	l	i	s	h	m	e	n	t
l	h	i	f	f	y	c	h	o	i	c	e	o	u
t	a	k	r	n	a	b	i	l	i	t	i	e	s
e	l	o	i	w	t	h	e	u	s	e	f	u	l
r	l	s	e	e	y	m	o	t	i	v	a	t	e
n	e	i	n	t	e	l	l	i	g	e	n	c	e
a	n	e	d	e	c	b	h	o	p	e	f	u	l
t	g	u	s	a	a	e	u	n	g	o	a	l	s
i	e	l	h	g	r	l	m	s	t	a	b	l	e
v	o	a	i	e	i	i	o	e	s	i	a	r	p
e	u	v	p	r	n	e	r	g	n	i	p	o	c
s	a	r	e	a	g	f	w	i	n	n	e	r	!

Message: __ __   __ __ __   __ __ __ __   __ __ __ __ __ ,

__ __ __   __ __ __   __   __ __ __ __ __ __ !

reproducible

Words That Work For You!

Extension Activities

Art

Have students make word posters. Each student writes words all over a sheet of art paper, using letters in a variety of sizes, colors, and shapes. Students should cover every possible space on their papers. Encourage them to use word groups that convey a specific emotion or idea.

Feeling Word Poster: angry, sad, content

Pressure Word Poster: quick, late, testing

Optimistic Word Poster: cheerful, happy, hopeful

Language Arts

- Discuss slang with your students. Explain that shortened language is often used when people are in a rush. For instance, instead of saying "Are you coming?", we sometimes say "Coming?" Ask students to give five more examples of shortened language. Here's a clue: Look at advertisements. Advertisers frequently use shortened language.
- Ask students to look up the word *honor.*
  1. How many syllables does the word have?
  2. How many different meanings does *honor* have?
  3. What is a synonym for *honor*?
  4. What is an antonym for *honor*?
  5. Give an example of an honorable thing you have done.

Math

Ask students to spend a few minutes listening to the speech of themselves and their friends. Encourage them to listen for "useless words" such as *yeah, okay, um, uh,* and *really*. Make a graph to record how often in a day students use these words. Challenge them to break the habit!

Science

The power of magnets is captivating. Magnets act in different ways. Magnets push away from each other. Magnets attract each other and other objects. Demonstrate with two magnets. Words can also attract and push away. Ask students to make a list of 20 words that attract them and 20 words that repel them.

Spin Away Pessimism

Lesson 4

Materials

Student copies of "Spin Away Pessimism!" (page 25)

Paper clip and pencil for each group

Student copies of "A Better Way to Say It" (page 26)

Objective: Students will find alternatives to negative statements.

Time Required: 45–60 minutes

Insights

Once you decide you are in control of your life, you will accomplish much more.

Negative words can influence your thinking. Avoid using these words and you can remain optimistic.

Self-awareness allows you to make changes.

When you want to change, it is because you have explored and gained insight.

Introduction

Introduce this activity by writing the following statement on the chalkboard: *We are victims of our speech habits*. Discuss with students what this statement means and how this idea affects them and the people around them. Give examples from George Bernard Shaw's *Pygmalion* —later made into a movie titled *My Fair Lady*—in which the main character's speech is altered and her life is changed.

Brainstorm some popular or common expressions. Ask students the following:

1. What words or phrases do people say that make them seem negative?
2. What words or phrases make them seem positive?
3. Have people said things to you that made you feel negative?
4. Could they have said these things in a way to make you feel more positive?

Spin Away Pessimism

Activity

Divide the class into groups of three. Hand out a "Spin Away Pessimism!" worksheet, tagboard, scissors, a hole punch, and a pushpin to each group. Read through the directions and allow students to play the game.

Anchoring

After groups have played the game, come together as a class. Ask students to share some of their positive statements. Discuss how changes in their speech habits could help them. Remind them to consciously practice using positive statements. To reinforce the use of positive speech, have students complete the "Better Way to Say It" worksheet. Remind them that they do not have to be victims of their own speech habits!

Name ____

Spin Away Pessimism!

Directions: Make a spinner by placing a pencil tip through the loop at one end of a paper clip. Place the spinner at the center of the dial. Flick the paper clip with your finger to spin it. To play the game, work in a group of three students. Players take turns spinning. On your turn, read the statement to which the spinner points and try to change it into a positive statement. If you can, you earn five points. If you can't, you earn no points. Play until time is up.

What can you say instead of . . .

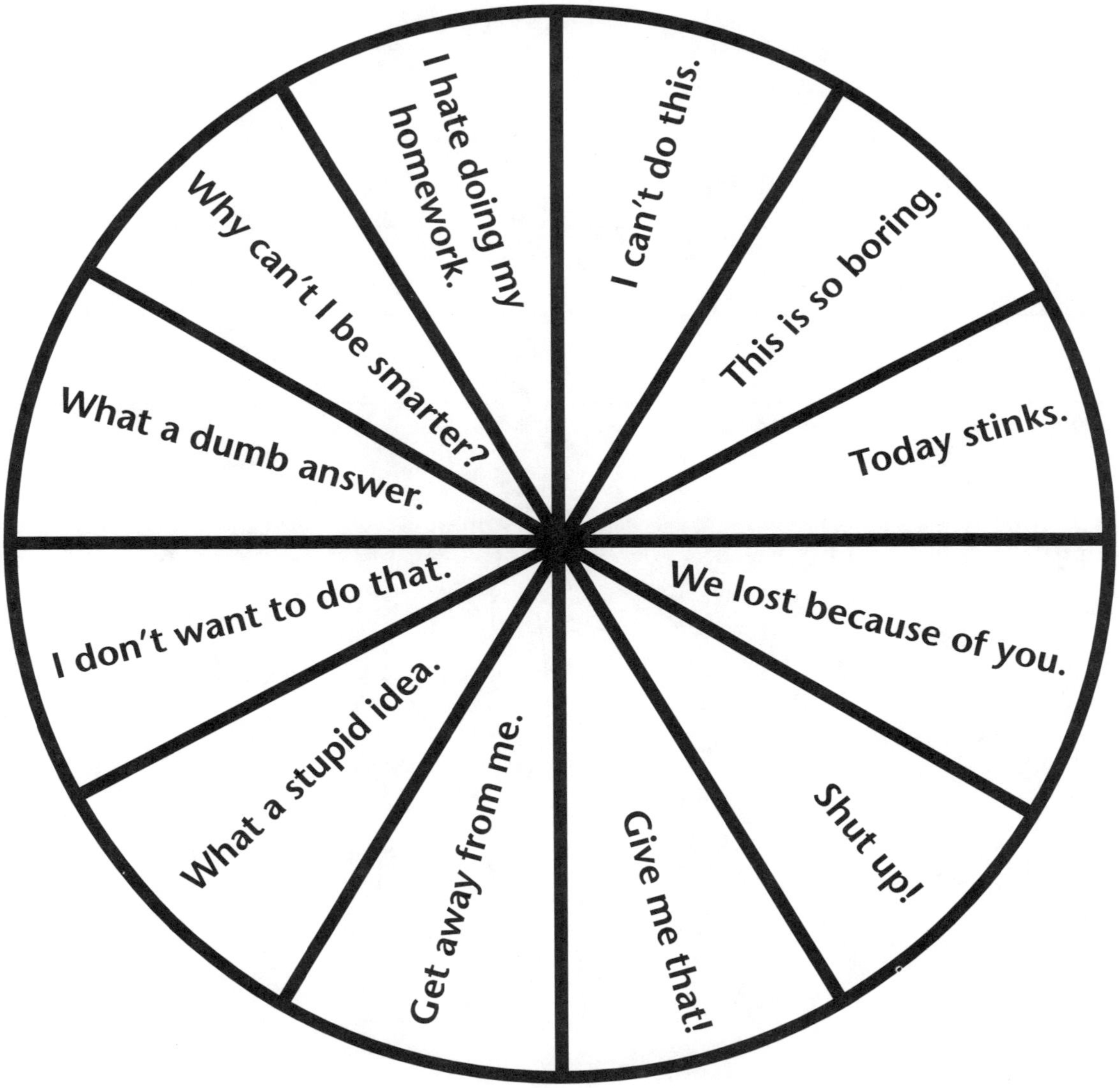

- I can't do this.
- This is so boring.
- Today stinks.
- We lost because of you.
- Shut up!
- Give me that!
- Get away from me.
- What a stupid idea.
- I don't want to do that.
- What a dumb answer.
- Why can't I be smarter?
- I hate doing my homework.

Name ____________________

A Better Way to Say It

Directions: Think about words or phrases that you use which may make you sound negative or make others feel pessimistic. Write these in the left column. Now think about how you can change what you say to sound more optimistic. Write the change in the right column. Practice using these new words and phrases.

Pessimistic Words or Phrases	**New Optimistic Words or Phrases**
1. ____________	1. ____________
2. ____________	2. ____________
3. ____________	3. ____________
4. ____________	4. ____________
5. ____________	5. ____________
6. ____________	6. ____________

Extension Activities

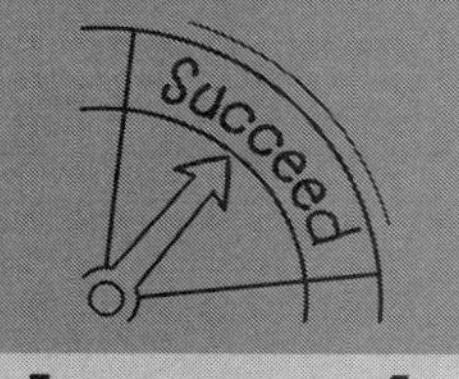

Language Arts

Ask each student to pretend that he or she is in charge of training a new Olympic runner. Have each student write a list of orders, using some of these words: *always, never, forever, can't, lose, fail.* Ask students to discuss how a runner might respond to this list. Next, have students write phrases using these words: *sometimes, maybe, can, together, goals, good effort.* Encourage students to read over both lists. Which words and phrases would be most useful to a good trainer?

Science

Ask the class to imagine that scientists have developed the first space station. The first group of space pioneers has been selected and your students are a part of the team. Ask students to describe one adventure in which the scientists are pessimistic about the journey. Then ask them to write another adventure in which the scientists are optimistic. To which group would students like to belong? Why?

Social Studies

Have students use atlases or maps to find 20 cities or other places that have optimistic-sounding names. Then ask students to complete the following tasks:

- Prepare a travel brochure to one of these places. Advertise all the positive activities and sights to see in this optimistic city or country.
- Write a story about an event that takes place in this city or country. Be sure the story reflects optimism and the events fit the name of place.

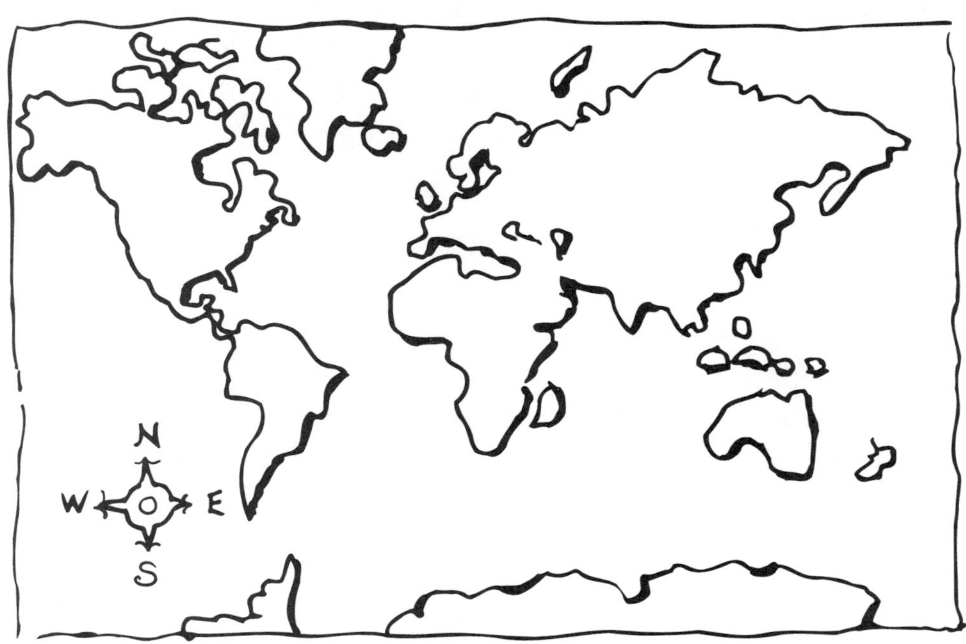

Lesson 5

Helplessness to Hopefulness

Materials

Student copies of "Bother, Bother " (page 30)

Student copies of "Hopeful, Not Helpless, Face-off" (page 31)

Objective: Students will work toward changing helpless attitudes into hopeful attitudes.

Time Required: 45 minutes

Insights

Take charge of your life. Learn how to motivate yourself.

Some words we use make us sound helpless. Become aware of these words and avoid them. Turn "helpless" into "hopeful."

Setting small goals leads to bigger success.

Put your goals down in writing. Let them serve as daily reminders of what you want to accomplish.

Introduction

Ask students to define the word *competition*. Lead a discussion about competition. Here are some are some questions to consider:

1. What are some of the ways our society is competitive?
2. What are some examples of competitive situations?
3. How do you feel when you know you have to compete against others?
4. Why do people compete?

Explain to students that competition can affect our attitudes. Our attitudes, in turn, can affect how often we are successful. When we are not successful, we need to alter our attitudes so we can be hopeful for success the next time.

Helplessness to Hopefulness

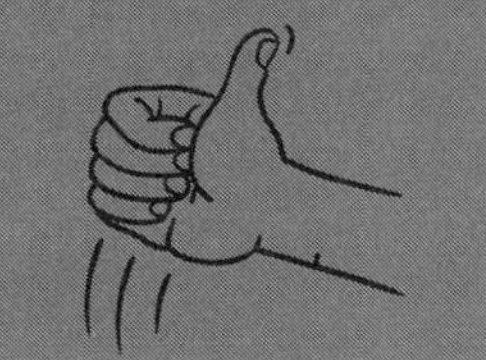

Activity

Give each student a copy of the "Bother, Bother" worksheet. Remind students that these worksheets are for their eyes only, so they should answer the questions as honestly as possible. Read the directions aloud and allow students time to respond to the questionnaires.

After students have completed the questionnaires, tell them they may keep their results private or share with the class any insights or comments they may have. Write the following statement on the chalkboard: *Sometimes we feel helpless, but we don't need to be hopeless.*

Allow time for discussion. Next, place students in pairs. Distribute a copy of the "Hopeful, Not Helpless, Face-off" worksheet to each group. Read the directions together. Allow students time to play the game.

Anchoring

After groups have finished, bring the class together as a group. Discuss which statements sounded the most familiar or were the most difficult to change.

Lesson 5

Name ____

Bother, Bother

Directions: Read each statement and place a check in the column that best describes how often you make that statement.

How often do you make these statements?

	Almost Never	**Sometimes**	**Often**
I hate school.			
I'm not happy.			
I have no friends.			
Everyone hates me.			
I can't do well on this.			
I don't want to try anything new.			
I feel like crying.			
I want to be alone.			
I make a lot of mistakes.			
I feel anxious.			
I'm not any good at this.			
I really don't care.			
No one really cares.			
I don't have a plan.			
I am not ready.			
I can't do this right.			
No one helps me.			
That's impossible.			
I can't handle this.			
I don't know what to do.			

If you answered mostly in the "Often" section, it's time to change the way you think.

Name ______________________________

Lesson 5

Hopeful, Not Helpless, Face-off

Directions: Partners face each other. One student makes the statement on the left. His or her partner responds using the sentence starter on the right or by making up a positive comment. Partners reverse roles halfway through the activity.

Partner 1 says:	**Partner 2 responds:**
1. I think I will just lie here for a few more minutes.	I wouldn't do that because . . .
2. I'm not very good at this.	You should . . .
3. I don't find anything funny.	You enjoy . . .
4. I know it won't work.	We'll have to try . . .
5. I don't know what to do.	Starting is . . .
6. I have too many problems.	I have problems too, but . . .
7. I hate everyone in this place.	I don't like everyone, but . . .
8. I'm so far behind, I'll never catch up.	I know you . . .
9. Everyone hates me.	Most people don't . . .
10. I never have enough time.	If you . . .

Change places with your partner.

Partner 2 says:	**Partner 1 responds:**
11. This is just too hard.	You have already . . .
12. Planning doesn't help.	How do you . . .
13. I never set goals.	What is a goal? Let me . . .
14. I don't know where to start.	Let's pretend this is . . .
15. I am always late.	First you should . . .
16. I am so depressed.	Can you think of . . .
17. I'm always so tired.	Try . . .
18. I keep losing everything.	Have you thought of . . .
19. I don't know a thing about that.	The library . . .
20. I don't really care about that.	What about the time . . .

Helplessness to Hopefulness

Extension Activities

Language Arts

- Have students list as many words as possible that encourage them and keep them on track.
- Ask students to write their favorite ways to avoid feeling helpless. Have class members share their responses.
- Using quotation books, the Internet, and other resources, ask students to find quotations about the following subjects: *optimism, love, hope, encouragement, helpfulness*. Have students design and decorate charts featuring these quotations. Display the charts around the room.
- Have students research the lives of famous individuals who had to overcome great odds to become successful. Possible choices include: Helen Keller, Harriet Tubman, George Washington Carver, Jackie Robinson, Tom Hanks, Gail Devers.
- Ask each class member to write a dialogue between two students. Have students choose at least three pessimistic statements from the "Hopeful, Not Helpless, Face-off" worksheet and use these phrases within the dialogue. Invite students to choose partners and act out their dialogues for the class.

Science

Inventors are hopeful that someday they will find the answers they are looking for. Ask students to find books about inventions or inventors. Have each student write or draw one invention, record the year it was created, and write a short paragraph about the inventor. What qualities are required to be an inventor?

Accept the Challenge!

Lesson 6

Materials

Student copies of "My Private Beliefs" (page 35)

Student copies of "Accept the Challenge!" (page 36)

Objective: Students will examine their personal belief systems and consider changes that will give them a more positive outlook.

Time Required: 45 minutes

Insights

Believe in yourself. You are what you believe.

Find your own positive mental energizers and use them.

Devise your own personal strategy to ward off negative or pessimistic thoughts.

We all have a choice. We can choose to be optimistic or pessimistic.

Introduction

Begin by writing the following sentences on the chalkboard: *You are what you believe. You can affect your life by changing your attitude.* Discuss with students what they think these two statements mean. Emphasize that their personal attitudes are governed by their inner belief systems. Explain to students that confronting these attitudes is a very private thing. They are the only ones who truly know their own beliefs. These beliefs affect their attitudes and also affect the way they handle the challenges they face. Ask these questions:

1. What is a belief?
2. How can our private beliefs give us support and help us?
3. In what ways can our private beliefs be detrimental to our success?
4. Where do our beliefs come from?

Lesson 6

Accept the Challenge!

Activity

Hand out copies of "My Private Beliefs." Allow time for students to complete and consider their answers. Remind them that examining their beliefs privately is the first step to growth.

After students have completed "My Private Beliefs," pass out copies of "Accept the Challenge!" Read the directions with students and allow them time to finish the worksheet.

Anchoring

After groups have finished, bring the class together as a group. Ask volunteers to share any of their belief goals with the group.

Name ____

My Private Beliefs

Directions: Read through the statements listed below. If you think the statement is true about you, circle TRUE. If you think it is not true about you, circle FALSE. Remember, this worksheet is for you to complete privately so that you can examine your personal beliefs.

1. I believe I can do anything I try.	TRUE	FALSE
2. I believe I am a nice person.	TRUE	FALSE
3. I believe I can make changes in myself.	TRUE	FALSE
4. I believe I am considerate of others' feelings.	TRUE	FALSE
5. I believe I am smart.	TRUE	FALSE
6. I believe I am friendly.	TRUE	FALSE
7. I believe I will be successful.	TRUE	FALSE
8. I believe I am fun to be with.	TRUE	FALSE
9. I believe there are lots of good people.	TRUE	FALSE
10. I believe things will get better.	TRUE	FALSE
11. I believe if I help someone, someone will help me.	TRUE	FALSE
12. I believe I am a hard worker.	TRUE	FALSE
13. I believe I can figure things out on my own.	TRUE	FALSE
14. I believe in saying I'm sorry.	TRUE	FALSE
15. I believe I have a good future ahead of me.	TRUE	FALSE

Count up all of your TRUE answers and compare them to the scores below.

12–15 Your beliefs make you optimistic and strong!

9–11 You are in good shape. Keep thinking positive.

5–8 Think about making some changes. Talk with someone you trust about your beliefs.

0–4 Talk to someone you trust to get help understanding your beliefs and why they need to change.

Lesson 6

Name ______________________________

Accept the Challenge!

Directions: Read the sentences below. If you agree with the statement, draw a star in front of the sentence. If you do not, leave it blank. Be honest with yourself so that you can begin to make positive changes.

I say "Good morning" to my family and friends.

I try to look my best.

Every day is a new day, and there are challenges to face.

I try to find solutions to problems as they occur.

I study hard and know I will do well on tests.

I try to help those around me when they need help.

I don't stay awake at night worrying about things.

When I feel depressed, I find something to do.

I enjoy taking the time to appreciate the beauty around me.

When I start to think depressing or angry thoughts, I have a way to stop them.

I set goals for myself.

I make plans when I am given an assignment.

I congratulate others when they do well.

I give myself encouragement when I try something new.

When I do solve a problem, I think about what I did so I can use the strategy again.

I treat others with respect.

I say "Please" and "Thank you."

I don't tease people about their mistakes.

I do not whine about things that don't go my way.

I take responsibility for things that are my fault.

15 or more stars—You have a strong belief system and positive outlook!

11 to 14 stars—You're doing well. Keep trying!

10 stars or less—It may be time to rethink your beliefs.

Now circle all the statements that you didn't star. Out of those, choose three that you would like to work on changing. Think about how you will accomplish these changes, and be ready to discuss them with the class.

Accept the Challenge!

Extension Activities

Language Arts

- Ask students to find biographies and autobiographies of famous people who have achieved success because of strong beliefs in themselves and their futures. Once each student has chosen an individual to research, have him or her write a short essay, explaining what the person accomplished and what made him or her strong. Encourage students to share their essays with the class. Ask the class to compare the traits of the various successful people they wrote about.
- Have students write "Dear Crabby" letters, pretending they are bitter, complaining individuals with problems. Then have them exchange their letters with a classmate. Now they are the advice columnist. They will answer their classmate's pessimistic letter by giving positive advice to help change his or her attitude and solve the problem.
- Ask students to work with partners to act out short skits in which one of the characters has a problem. The other character in the skit has to help make a plan that will solve the problem.
- Have your class design posters that promote optimistic sayings. Encourage them to use colorful graphics and bold lettering. Display their posters around the school and classroom.

Lesson 7

Get the Bugs Out

Materials

Student copies of "It Really Bugs Me" (page 40)

Student copies of "Mental Energizers" (page 41)

Objective: Students will learn to recognize their pet peeves. Once they are able to recognize them, students will practice techniques to deal with the stress these annoyances create.

Time Required: 30 minutes

Insights

Taking time to analyze the things that bother you gives insight on how to deal with those pet peeves.

When you allow yourself to react to pet peeves, you put yourself under stress.

Learn to refocus your attention away from the things that annoy you.

Practice relaxation techniques, such as breathing, that help get you past stressful situations.

Introduction

Ask students to share any special talents they have, such as tongue-rolling, double-jointed digits, unusual sounds, or wiggling ears. Allow everyone to share, but be aware of any looks of disgust or annoyance.

Get the Bugs Out

Activity

Explain to students that some of these talents are unusual or funny, but sometimes they really annoy other people. Particularly annoying habits or situations are sometimes called "pet peeves." Share one of your own pet peeves with students. For example, maybe it annoys you when students take paper from the middle of the stack instead of from the top. Ask students to share some of their pet peeves, reminding them not to name specific people.

Give each student a copy of the "It Really Bugs Me" worksheet. Read the directions with them and allow time for completion. Ask students to share some of their responses. Note that not all people are bothered by the same things. Remind students that we can't be responsible for other people; we can only be responsible for ourselves. Therefore, we must come up with our own mental energizers, or ways to deal with our pet peeves when we encounter them. Pass out the "Mental Energizers" worksheets. Review the directions, and have students complete the worksheets.

Anchoring

Assemble as a class and ask for volunteers to share the mental energizers that they are going to try the next time they face a stressful situation.

Lesson 7

Name ______________________________

It Really Bugs Me

Directions: Read the sentence starters below. Write your responses in the spaces provided. Be as descriptive as possible, but, to avoid hurt feelings, remember not to aim any of your pet peeves at specific people.

1. I really lose my temper when . . .

____

2. It bothers my ears when I hear . . .

____

3. It makes me feel ill when I see . . .

____

4. It makes me feel bad when . . .

____

5. I can't stand to remain in the room when . . .

____

6. I am bothered by the feel of . . .

____

7. I am bugged by the scent of . . .

____

Name ____

Mental Energizers

Directions: Read and compare the following list of mental energizers. With a partner, discuss each one and how it helps minimize stress. Rank them in order from 1 to 10, with 1 being the most important mental energizer you will use.

____ Plan a new strategy in my mind.

____ Write my thoughts down in a journal.

____ Close my eyes and take five deep, slow breaths.

____ Refocus by humming or singing quietly to myself.

____ Draw a picture or cartoon.

____ Hold a memento in my hand and study it.

____ Remember a happy or funny moment.

____ Flex and relax my hands.

____ Close my eyes and daydream.

____ Change the subject or the scenery that is bugging me.

Add your own ideas on the lines below:

____

____

____

____

____

Remember, the things that bug you are particular to you. Find ways to deal with your pet peeves to avoid stress, anger, or frustration.

Extension Activities

Art

- Promote laughter in your classroom. Invite students to make posters that feature their favorite riddles or jokes. Hang the posters where everyone can enjoy them.
- Ask students to make comic strips that show examples of stressful situations. The comics should depict characters dealing with these situations by using mental energizers to minimize stress.

Language Arts

Have students write letters about their pet peeves and how they are going to deal with them. Encourage students to be specific about how they think their solutions will work. Students may decide to keep the letters to themselves or share them with their families and friends.

Math

- As a teacher, are messy math papers one of your pet peeves? Ask students to help you avoid this annoyance by making an effort to be neat with their work. Encourage them to use columns and double spaces or draw boxes around their final answers. Alternatively, students can use graph paper and write a single digit in each square. Ask students to help you devise a plan to eliminate messy papers. Offer reinforcement to students who utilize the plan.
- Divide the class into student pairs. Have each student make a list of his or her pet peeves. Then have students work with their partners to place the pet peeves in a Venn diagram. The diagram should show the pet peeves students share as well as the pet peeves unique to each student.

Good Humor Day

Lesson 8

Materials

Writing paper for each student

Watch or clock with second hand

Student copies of "Humor Survival Kit" (page 45)

Objective: Students will learn about the value of humor.

Time Required: 45 minutes

Insights

Do not take yourself too seriously. Learn to laugh at yourself.

To be able to appreciate humor in life, you must be willing to accept life's imperfections.

Think of a moment from the past that puts a smile on your face. Keep that memory handy for those times when you could really use a laugh.

Sarcasm and put-downs are not humorous. They are damaging to other people's optimism.

Introduction

Write the following statements on the chalkboard and discuss them with students:

Laughter is a bodily function precious to health.
Laughter enhances your looks.
Laughter releases stress built up in the body.

Brainstorm words that trigger humor. Write these on the chalkboard.

Lesson 8

Good Humor Day

Activity

Examine the effects of humor on your heart rate. Assign partners to check one another's pulse rates. Give instructions for taking pulse rates using two fingers placed gently on a pulse point such as the wrist or neck. One partner counts each pulse while the other counts 10 seconds on a clock. Multiply the pulse count by six to get the beats per minute. Instruct each partner to take a resting pulse rate and record it on paper. The rates will probably be around 90 beats per minute. An adult's resting pulse rate is about 70 beats per minute.

Have students get into larger groups that include their partners. Students will compose alliteration tongue-twisters using their own names, and record them on writing paper. Remind students to make their tongue-twisters as silly and funny as possible, but they also must remain positive and appropriate for a school setting. Example: *Rambling Robert rapidly ran rings round the resting rhinoceros.*

When students are finished, ask them to share their tongue-twisters within their groups. After bumbles, laughter, and giggles, ask partners to take their pulse rates again. The pulse rates should have increased as a result of the laughter. Ask students if there are other situations in which pulse rates increase, such as exercise. Explain that laughter is like exercise, because it's good for us.

Tell students that they will design "humor survival kits" to help them stay optimistic. Hand out the "Humor Survival Kit" worksheet and read directions with students. Have them list 10 things that are sure to make them smile. These can include things like a silly song or a videotape of a funny television show.

Anchoring

After students have had time to work on their kits, bring the class together as a group. Discuss the following questions:

1. Why is laughter important to our health?
2. What makes you laugh?
3. How can we make others laugh?
4. What happens when one person starts to laugh when no one else is laughing?

Remind students that nothing can change a bad attitude faster than a good laugh.

Name ______________________________

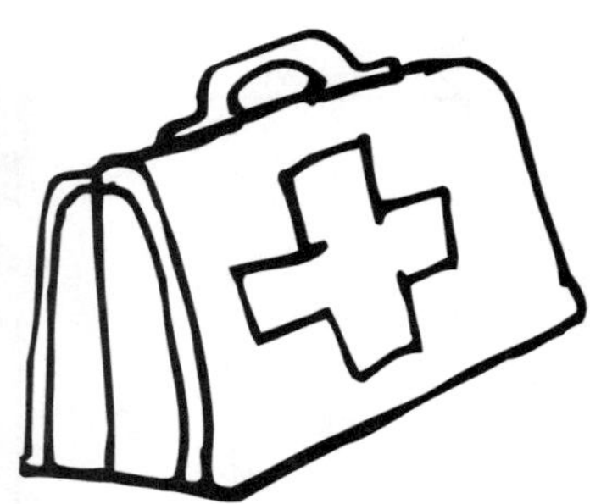

Humor Survival Kit

Directions: What would belong in your personal Humor Survival Kit? What 10 things are sure to get you giggling? Design a Humor Survival Kit for times when you need a good laugh. That way, when you need some emergency comic relief, you'll know where to look.

1. ______________________________
2. ______________________________
3. ______________________________
4. ______________________________
5. ______________________________
6. ______________________________
7. ______________________________
8. ______________________________
9. ______________________________
10. ______________________________

Lesson 8

Good Humor Day

Extension Activities

Art

- Ask students to make sentence strips from the tongue-twisters they wrote earlier. Have students print these out in colorful lettering. Hang the decorated strips throughout the classroom or on a bright bulletin board.
- Have the class brainstorm a list of silly words or phrases. Let each student pick a phrase to illustrate on a large index card. Punch holes in the tops of the cards and hang them from the ceiling with string.

Language Arts

- Ask students to write a series of "smiling similes." Explain that a simile is a figure of speech that uses the word *like* or *as* to compare two dissimilar objects. Encourage students to make their similes as positive, yet as silly, as they can. Example: *He is as calm as a candle flame in a tornado.*
- Have students assemble Humor Survival Kits using their lists from the worksheet. Encourage students to include all the actual items they can find. For example, they might include videotaped reruns of their favorite television shows or copies of funny comic strips. Have students use their imaginations to design representations of items they can't find or make.
- Create a Laughter Collection Book. Ask students to invite their friends and families to contribute jokes and riddles that can be collected together into a book and displayed in your classroom.
- According to a famous old saying: "Laughter is the best medicine." Ask each student to write a brief paragraph about what this phrase means to him or her.
- Have each student research the life and times of a famous comedian, then write an illustrated report on this person. Have students share famous jokes or skits they have learned while researching these comedians.

Music

Have students help you find songs that have humorous titles or words. Make a list of these songs and listen to them or sing them with your class.

The Power of Image

Lesson 9

Materials

Assortment of magazine advertisements, particularly those aimed at the young adult market

Student copies of "The Power of Advertising" (page 49)

Thesaurus or dictionary

Objective: Students will gain an understanding of the power of images and words through the medium of advertising. They will be able to analyze advertisers' sales pitches and learn to react thoughtfully rather than emotionally.

Time Required: 45 minutes

Insights

It's important to know the power of words and images and how they affect our attitudes.

Your communication skills should be clear. Know what you want to say. Understand what is said to you.

Make your communication work for you.

Introduction

Before beginning this activity, take a quick visual check of your students, and observe what types of brand-name merchandise seem to be popular. Bring these brands to the attention of the class. Discuss with students the reasons for purchasing these brand-name items. List some of these reasons on the chalkboard. Display a magazine advertisement. Discuss the following:

1. What is this advertisement trying to sell?
2. What images are used in the ad?
3. What words are used? Are these words common or unusual?
4. What ideas are being presented about the product?

Point out to the class how ads use stylish words and images to associate particular ideas or lifestyles with the products being advertised. Ask students to come up with other ways to advertise the product in the displayed ad.

Lesson 9

The Power of Image

Activity

Ask students to work in small groups. Give each group a magazine advertisement. Each group should also have a copy of "The Power of Advertising" worksheet. Read the directions with students and answer any questions they may have. Allow each group to complete the worksheet.

Anchoring

Have each group share and discuss their findings with the rest of the class. Discuss whether this activity will affect why they decide to purchase certain items in the future.

Name ______________________________________

The Power of Advertising

Directions: Use one of the advertisements supplied by your teacher. Discuss with your group the following questions. Jot down your ideas in the space below.

1. What product is being sold?

   ____

2. What is the name of the company that manufactures the product?

   ____

3. What images or pictures are used in the ad?

   ____

4. What words does the ad use?

   ____

5. Use a dictionary or thesaurus to rewrite the advertisement's message in different words. What does it really say?

   ____

6. What ideas or messages are promoted in the advertisement?

   ____

7. Does the ad make any promises, either obvious or hidden, about what this product will do for you?

   ____

8. Would you buy this product based on this ad? Why or why not?

   ____

The Power of Image

Extension Activities

Language Arts

- Review synonyms with the class. Next, ask each student to choose a simple descriptive word like *pretty, sad, happy, big, small, ugly, quiet*, or *noisy*. Have students find the words in a thesaurus, then make a list of all the synonyms shown for the words. Instruct students to write sentences using each synonym. Explain that every word conveys a unique image, even if its meaning is similar to that of another word. For this reason, word choice is very important in writing.
- Have each student select a character from a novel he or she has read. Ask students to "advertise" these characters by describing his or her characteristics using vivid and powerful words.
- Instruct students to describe a real location using expressive and colorful language.
- Ask students to imagine that they are reporters. The newspaper has asked them to interview two people who have seen a UFO. As a class, brainstorm a list of interview questions to ask the witnesses. Then have each student write a newspaper report on the event using the "answers" to these questions.
- Sometimes, advertisements can be deceiving. Ask students if they have ever been disappointed in a product because it did not live up to its advertisement. Instruct students to write paragraphs about their experiences.

Math

As homework, have students make a tally of the number and types of commercials shown during a favorite program. Ask students to divide the advertisements into simple groupings, such as commercials for kids and commercials for adults. Have students graph their results and share them with the class.

Social Studies

Another type of advertisement is the public service announcement. These differ from regular advertising in that they are designed to promote messages for the public good, such as no smoking or drug awareness, rather than to sell a product. Ask students to discuss the public service announcements they have seen. Did the public service announcements do a good job "selling" their ideas?

Let's Advertise Optimism!

Lesson 10

Materials

Student copies of "Optimism: The Choice Is Right"(page 52)

Objective: Students will use the concepts of advertising to "sell" optimism to other students.

Time Required: Planning time: 30 minutes
Project time: one or more hours

Insights

Practice makes perfect.

Laugh and the whole world laughs with you.

Happiness is contagious.

A positive outlook is worth passing on to others—think of what we could accomplish together!

Optimism is the catalyst to success.

Introduction

Review the concepts of advertising discussed in the last lesson. Now students have the opportunity to apply what they have learned and pass it on to others. Discuss with students the different ways they might advertise optimism throughout the school.

Activity

Divide the class into groups. Hand out an "Optimism: The Choice Is Right" worksheet to each group. Give the groups time to discuss and plan what they will be doing to sell optimism to other students. The amount of time necessary for project completion will depend on the type of project selected.

Anchoring

Establish a project completion date. At that time, allow students to display or present their optimism salesmanship.

Name ______________________________

Optimism: The Choice Is Right

Get ready to advertise what you know about the power of optimism.

Directions: With your group, choose from the following list of project ideas to promote optimism to others in your school. Once you have selected a project, begin brainstorming with group members to decide what supplies you will need to complete your project. Don't forget to determine which group member will be responsible for each task. Then estimate how long you think it will take you to complete your project.

1. Plan a mural on optimistic people or an optimistic dream.
2. Write a poem about optimism.
3. Plan an advertisement for the local newspaper.
4. Prepare a script for a radio station. It can be informational or dramatic.
5. Prepare a play about optimism.
6. Start an optimist newsletter for your school.
7. Prepare daily optimistic quotations. Ask the principal if these can be read to the school each morning.
8. Start an Optimism Club. Begin by writing out the rules of the club and the goals you want to achieve. How will you advertise for members?

Your Plan: ______________________________

Supplies needed: ______________________________

____

____

____

____

____

____

____

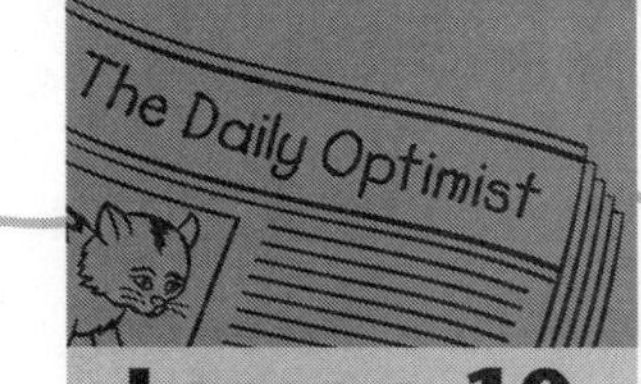

Let's Advertise Optimism!

Extension Activities

Language Arts

- Ask students to write letters to the editor of your local newspaper about your class optimism project. Invite the newspaper to interview your class.
- Have each student write a letter to an adult in the school or community. The letter should explain what the student has learned about the importance of optimism. It might also ask the adult to share his or her insights on optimism.
- Encourage students to find the names of authors who have written books on optimism. Have students write letters to one of these authors letting him or her know what the class has accomplished.

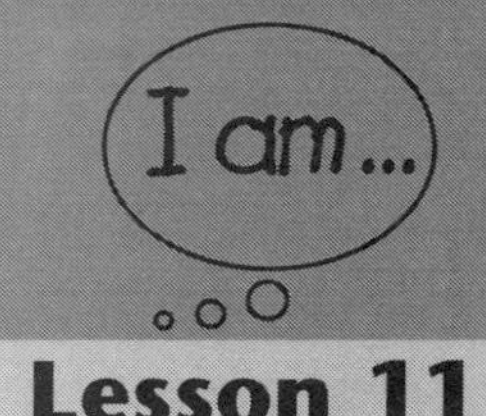

Lesson 11

What's the Size of Your Optimism?

Materials

Student copies of "Size Up Your Optimism" (page 55)

Objective: As they prepare for the culmination of this unit on optimism, students will reflect on what they have learned and how much they have applied to their lives.

Time Required: 45 minutes

Insights

Take time to reflect on what you've learned and how you have applied it to your life.

Concentrate on what you do well.

Focus on the good things in life.

Make a list of the things you do well. Remind yourself that these are your personal assets.

Introduction

Explain to students that this is a time to share their successes. Each student should be prepared to tell of one good thing that has happened to him or her in the last few days.

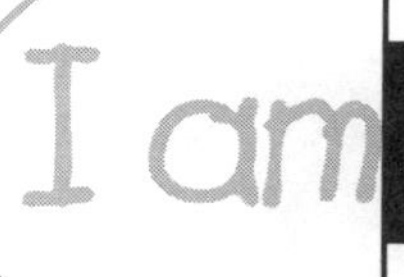

Activity

Hand out copies of "Size Up Your Optimism" to students. Read over the directions with them. Students should work privately on this part of the activity.

Anchoring

Point out that once they have completed the worksheets, students have a set of goals to serve as a reminder of what they want to accomplish. These goals can help students remain on the positive track.

Name ______________________________________

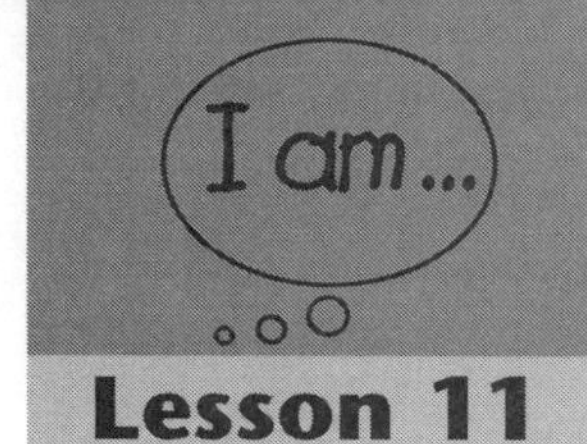

Size Up Your Optimism

Directions: Below are 10 statements related to optimism. Read each statement. In the space provided, give an example from your life where you have demonstrated the action in the statement. Give examples for as many statements as you can. When finished, find out your optimism "score."

1. I have a positive attitude. ______________________
2. I am considerate and respectful of others. ______________________
3. I set goals for myself and work to accomplish them. ______________________
4. I forgive people. ______________________
5. If I don't succeed, I try another approach. ______________________
6. I like to try new things. ______________________
7. I look at the humorous side of things and remain in a good mood. ______________________
8. When I am angry, anxious, or sad, I use a mental energizer. ______________________
9. I am proud of my personal appearance. ______________________
10. I believe in myself and what I can do. ______________________

10 examples	Excellent! You are applying what you learn.
7–9 examples	You are off to a good beginning. Keep up the positive thoughts!
4–6 examples	You're making an effort. Keep thinking positively.
3 or less	Reflect on what you can change. Talk to others about new ideas.

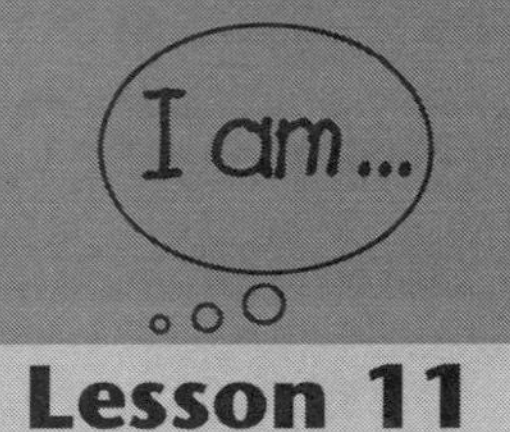

What's the Size of Your Optimism?

Extension Activities

Art

- Throughout the centuries, artists have painted dragons any way they wish because dragons are imaginary creatures. Ask each student to draw a dragon that is optimistic and one that is pessimistic. How will they be different?
- Have students design flags which represent themselves. Each flag should display its designer's positive characteristics using colorful graphics.
- Instruct each student to draw a tree with many branches. On each branch, the student should write one of the optimistic words that he or she has learned during the unit.

Language Arts

- A portrait artist usually paints what a person looks like. Have students "paint" portraits with words. Ask each student to write a word portrait about his or her best friend. The portrait should describe what the friend looks like, plus tell about any special characteristics the friend has.
- Encourage students to participate in a free-association activity by giving them the following directions: Look at any picture. Jot down your thoughts and feelings as they are triggered by the picture. Let your mind wander. Give it the freedom to see different perspectives.
- Trying is important. Invite students to list some things that are worth trying that will bring them confidence, success, or happiness.
- Get a book on names from the library. Let students look up the meanings of their own names, including their first and middle names. Have them make posters of their names using attractive lettering and graphics.

Math

Discuss accounting with your class. Point out that assets and liabilities play a major role in business. Have students research the purpose of a profit and loss statement. Discuss how this relates to optimism and pessimism.

Join the Optimist Club!

Lesson 12

Materials

Student copies of "The Optimist's Pledge" (page 58)

Student copies of "The Optimist's Oath" (page 59)

Objective: Students will complete the Optimist's Pledge and recite the Optimist's Oath to demonstrate what they have learned about optimism.

Time Required: 45 minutes

Insights

Optimism: a cheerful frame of mind that enables a tea kettle to sing when it is filled with hot water.

An optimist sees an opportunity in every calamity; a pessimist sees a calamity in every opportunity.

Introduction

Congratulate students on the completion of this unit on optimism. Ask for examples of what they have learned from the activities in this unit. Discuss what was the most useful for different individuals.

Activity

Explain that in order to work on remaining optimistic, students will fill out a pledge, or promise, to remind them of their goals. Students will also recite an oath that reinforces the lessons learned in the unit. Hand out "The Optimist's Pledge" worksheet. Read over the directions and allow students time to complete the pledge on their own.

Anchoring

Once the pledges are completed and signed, hand out "The Optimist's Oath." Recite the oath together. Encourage students to review the oath often, as a reminder of all the rewards an optimistic attitude can bring.

Lesson 12

Name ______________________________

The Optimist's Pledge

Directions: Read the optimistic goals below. Choose two that you will pledge to work toward in the upcoming year. Answer the questions below each goal. Be sure to sign your name at the bottom of the pledge.

1. I will set specific goals for myself.
2. I will try to have a positive outlook.
3. I will have a personal belief that the best is yet to come.
4. I will try to show forgiveness.
5. I will have an optimistic attitude to help me succeed.
6. I will try to keep busy when I feel I am getting upset or depressed.
7. I will try to be cheerful even if I can't always be happy.

First Goal: ______________________________

How am I going to achieve this goal? ______________________________

Why is it important to me? ______________________________

How will this affect my future? ______________________________

Second Goal: ______________________________

How am I going to achieve this goal? ______________________________

Why is it important to me? ______________________________

How will this affect my future? ______________________________

Student Signature: ______________________________ Date: ______________

Teacher Signature: ______________________________ Grade: ______________

The Optimist's Oath

Read this oath together with your class.

I promise that I shall adopt an optimistic attitude.

I will plan my day as though good things will happen.

I will learn to set goals and solve problems.

I will practice my mental energizers during times of stress.

I will forgive others.

I will compliment others and accept compliments gracefully.

I will look for the best in all of my friends.

I will stop and think positively.

I will not use negative language.

I will not think negative thoughts about myself.

I will find constructive activities to occupy my time.

I will examine my appearance and look my best.

I will listen and reflect.

I know I will have a good life!

Answers for Student Worksheets

Page 12 **Changing Your Word Scenery**
Message: Celebrate change!

Page 16 **The Voice in Your Head**
Accept all reasonable answers.

Page 20 **Words That Work**

1. Antonyms for unprepared: *prepared, completed, goal-oriented*
2. Synonyms for sincere: *truthful, honest*
3. Antonyms for depressed: *cheerful, happy, hopeful*
4. Antonyms for negative: *positive, optimistic*
5. Synonyms for eager: *willing, enthusiastic, helpful*
6. Synonyms for hopeful: *eager, willing, enthusiastic*
7. Synonyms for intelligent: *smart, alert, quick, bright, brilliant*
8. Synonyms for optimistic: *positive, hopeful, enthusiastic*
9. Antonyms for slow: *fast, quick, alert, eager*
10. Synonyms for courage: *fearlessness, bravery*
11. Antonyms for inflexible: *flexible, adjustable*
12. Antonyms for inaccurate: *accurate, precise*
13. Synonyms for succeed: *accomplish, win, achieve*
14. Synonyms for grateful: *thankful, appreciative*
15. Synonyms for focus: *concentrate, attentive*
16. Antonyms for unmotivated: *motivated, goal-oriented*
17. Antonyms for pessimistic: *optimistic, positive*
18. Antonyms for fail: *succeed, win, accomplish, achieve*
19. Synonyms for generous: *giving, sharing*
20. Synonyms for cheerful: *happy, positive, optimistic*
21. Antonyms for hopeless: *hopeful, enthusiastic*
22. Synonyms for stable: *trustworthy, dependable*
23. Synonyms for confident: *sure, positive, hopeful*
24. Synonyms for humorous: *funny, witty, joking*
25. Synonyms for sad: *happy, cheerful*

Page 21 **Magic Words of Success**
Message: If you know these, you are a winner!

Pages 25, 26 **Spin Away Pessimism and A Better Way to Say It**
Accept all reasonable positive answers.

Page 31 **Hopeful, Not Helpless, Face-off**
Accept all reasonable positive answers.

Page 40 **It Really Bugs Me!**
Accept any answers that apply to students personally.

Page 45 **Humor Survival Kit**
Accept any answers that make the kit humorous.

Page 49 **The Power of Advertising**
Accept any answers appropriate to the advertisement.

Page 55 **Size Up Your Optimism**
Accept any examples students are able to relate.

Glossary of Terms

advertisement: a public notice or announcement, usually of something for sale

asset: anything that has value to a particular individual; a valuable or desirable thing to have

belief: a conviction that certain things are true

catalyst: something that serves to start a reaction

communication: the giving or exchange of information

constructive: helping to build; leading to improvement

destructive: tending to cause destruction; tearing down

experience: knowledge gained by having lived through something

focus: any center of activity; attention

frustration: the state of being prevented from reaching a goal

graphology: the study of handwriting

humorous: funny, amusing, comical

idiom: an accepted phrase or expression having a different meaning from what it literally says

image: a concept of a person or product held by the general public

inflexible: stiff, rigid, unyielding

insight: the ability to see and understand clearly the inner nature of things

internal dialogue: a manner of thinking about and discussing issues within one's self

liabilities: something that works to one's disadvantage

mental energizers: techniques that relieve the body and mind of stress

motivate: to encourage into action

optimism: the tendency to take the most hopeful view of situations

optimist: a person who thinks optimistically

passive: inactive; offering no resistance

pessimism: the tendency to always expect the worst

pessimist: a person who always expects the worst

pet peeve: a particular or special annoyance

pressure: a state of distress; a compelling influence

public service announcement: an informational commercial developed for the public good

sarcasm: a taunting remark, often ironical in nature

self-improvement: the act of aspiring to make one's self better through actions or thoughts

Related Resources

The following are books that support the theme of positive thinking. Share them with your students to enhance any of the lessons presented in this book.

The Best of Free Spirit: Five Years of Award-Winning News and Views on Growing Up by the Free Spirit Editors (Free Spirit Press, 1995).

Brain Quest: Be a Know It All by Chris Welles Feder and Mel Juffe (Workman Publishing, 1995).

Chicken Soup for the Kid's Soul: 101 Stories of Courage, Hope, and Laughter by Jack Canfield, Mark Victor Hansen, Patty Hansen, and Irene Dunlap (Health Communications, Inc., 1998).

Every Kid's Guide to Decision Making and Problem Solving by Joy Berry (Children's Press, 1987).

1,400 Things for Kids to Be Happy About: The Happy Book by Barbara Ann Kipfer (Workman, 1994).

Getting Your Message Across by Kathlyn Gay (New Discovery, 1993).

The Kid's Guide to Social Action: How to Solve the Social Problems You Choose and Turn Creative Thinking into Positive Action by Barbara A. Lewis, Pamela Espeland, and Caryn Pernu (Free Spirit, 1998).

Positive Thinking Every Day: An Inspiration for Each Day of the Year by Norman Vincent Peale (Simon & Schuster Trade, 1993).

The Power of Positive Thinking by Norman Vincent Peale (Fawcett Book Group, 1996).

Optimist of the Week

Awarded to

____

on ______________________________
(date)

Signed by

____

To: ______________________________

I like your attitude!
Keep up the good work!

From: ______________________________

Keep your face in the sunshine and you cannot see the shadow.

—Helen Keller

This award is presented to ____________________________

for keeping a sunny outlook on life.

Signed by ____________________________

To look up and not down,
To look forward and not back,
To look out and not in,
And to lend a hand.

—Edward Everett Hale

This award is presented to ____________________________

for being an optimist and giving a helping hand.

Signed by ____________________________